MK
175

Variety Photoplays

Also by Edward Field

Stand Up, Friend, With Me

(Lamont Award 1962)

Variety Photoplays

by Edward Field

Grove Press Inc.,
New York,

Some of these poems were first published in
*Book Week, Colorado State Review, Evergreen Review,
The Nation, The New York Review of Books, Southern
Poetry Review.*

Library of Congress Catalog Card Number: 67-20051

Second Printing

Manufactured in the United States of America

For my friends

Leah Schaefer
and
Alfred Chester

Contents

Part One: Old Movies

Part Two: Selected Short Subjects

PART ONE:
OLD MOVIES

Curse of the Cat Woman

It sometimes happens
that the woman you meet and fall in love with
is of that strange Transylvanian people
with an affinity for cats.

You take her to a restaurant, say, or a show,
on an ordinary date, being attracted
by the glitter in her slitty eyes and her catlike walk,
and afterwards of course you take her in your arms
and she turns into a black panther
and bites you to death.

Or perhaps you are saved in the nick of time
and she is tormented by the knowledge of her tendency:
That she daren't hug a man
unless she wants to risk clawing him up.

This puts you both in a difficult position—
panting lovers who are prevented from touching
not by bars but by circumstance:
You have terrible fights and say cruel things
for having the hots does not give you a sweet temper.

One night you are walking down a dark street
and hear the pad-pad of a panther following you,
but when you turn around there are only shadows,
or perhaps one shadow too many.

You approach, calling, "Who's there?"
and it leaps on you.
Luckily you have brought along your sword
and you stab it to death.

11

And before your eyes it turns into the woman you love,
her breast impaled on your sword,
her mouth dribbling blood saying she loved you
but couldn't help her tendency.

So death released her from the curse at last,
and you knew from the angelic smile on her dead face
that in spite of a life the devil owned,
love had won, and heaven pardoned her.

Frankenstein

The monster has escaped from the dungeon
where he was kept by the Baron,
who made him with knobs sticking out from each side of his
    neck
where the head was attached to the body
and stitching all over
where parts of cadavers were sewed together.

He is pursued by the ignorant villagers,
who think he is evil and dangerous because he is ugly
and makes ugly noises.
They wave firebrands at him and cudgels and rakes,
but he escapes and comes to the thatched cottage
of an old blind man playing on the violin Mendelssohn's
    "Spring Song."

Hearing him approach, the blind man welcomes him:
"Come in, my friend," and takes him by the arm.
"You must be weary," and sits him down inside the house.
For the blind man has long dreamed of having a friend
to share his lonely life.

The monster has never known kindness—the Baron was cruel—
but somehow he is able to accept it now,
and he really has no instincts to harm the old man,
for in spite of his awful looks he has a tender heart:
Who knows what cadaver that part of him came from?

The old man seats him at table, offers him bread,
and says, "Eat, my friend." The monster
rears back roaring in terror.
"No, my friend, it is good. Eat—gooood"
and the old man shows him how to eat,
and reassured, the monster eats

13

and says, "Eat—gooood,"
trying out the words and finding them good too.

The old man offers him a glass of wine,
"Drink, my friend. Drink—gooood."
The monster drinks, slurping horribly, and says,
"Drink—gooood," in his deep nutty voice
and smiles maybe for the first time in his life.

Then the blind man puts a cigar in the monster's mouth
and lights a large wooden match that flares up in his face.
The monster, remembering the torches of the villagers,
recoils, grunting in terror.
"No, my friend, smoke—gooood,"
and the old man demonstrates with his own cigar.
The monster takes a tentative puff
and smiles hugely, saying, "Smoke—gooood,"
and sits back like a banker, grunting and puffing.

Now the old man plays Mendelssohn's "Spring Song" on the
      violin
while tears come into our dear monster's eyes
as he thinks of the stones of the mob, the pleasures of meal-
      time,
the magic new words he has learned
and above all of the friend he has found.

It is just as well that he is unaware—
being simple enough to believe only in the present—
that the mob will find him and pursue him
for the rest of his short unnatural life,
until trapped at the whirlpool's edge
he plunges to his death.

She

You are on an expedition for a museum
following rumors of a lost civilization
in the Far North among the ice mountains.

You come across a block of ice
with a saber-tooth tiger frozen in it like a sentinel
and you know you are near.
For with a supply of fresh-frozen meat like that
man can survive in these parts.
Then you find frozen in the ice
some earlier explorers who disappeared.
The expression on their faces says
nothing pleasant is ahead.

A convenient avalanche opens a passageway
that leads into the lost kingdom.
You are seized and brought before the queen,
SHE, a young and beautiful girl.

You see her and love her,
and SHE wants you to rule forever at her side,
so SHE shows you her secret,
a magic fire that keeps her young,
for SHE is really a thousand years old, SHE confesses.
SHE has to step into the fire once a year:
It's time right now in fact.

You realize you have been taken in by an old lady,
you, who are only capable of loving youth—
and anyway SHE's no virgin, having had as many lovers as
      years
and killing them finally when SHE was tired of them.
Really, was it the new lovers or the fire that kept her young?

15

SHE said, "Wait a minute while I take my annual fire bath."
You are horrified—SHE is a monster and a tyrant—
and you stamp out the fire,
and before your eyes time catches up with her
and SHE ages into a hag, that beauty you just kissed,
crumples, dies, rots, dries up, and turns to dust,
a thousand years passing before your eyes.

No time to lose, for time was catching up with the kingdom
        too:
You make your escape to the present
just as the corridors of ice crash down behind you
obliterating once and for all all trace of SHE and her world,
and you stand safely outside on the edge of that avalanche.

Back in London at the museum
you stand around with colleagues in evening clothes
in front of a glass case holding a stuffed saber-tooth tiger.
"Magnificent specimen, that," Lord Avon says.
"Let me tell you the story," you say.
"Perhaps you will find it unbelievable but every word is true,"
as a mist of memory, of youth forever lost,
comes over your blue eyes.

Lower East Side: The George Bernstein Story

It starts on the Lower East Side
when Irving Berlin, Fanny Brice, Paul Muni,
all the bigshots in show business, the underworld,
politics, and the arts,
were still rollerskating among the pushcarts,
and calling up Hey Ma for a penny to be thrown down
and if no penny fell, going off to earn one by their talents.

Just off the boat the Bernsteins arrive,
corner Delancey and Orchard, greenhorns,
Mama with her big pot,
Papa looking for a sweatshop to work in,
and the kids Sammy and Ethel saying Gee Whiz
and eating their first bananas that tasted funny to them.

They settle in a cold-water flat
(nine dollars a month in those days—
now ninety if you qualify professional)
in a tenement that is multiracial rather than interracial
(meaning No Colored),
with an Irish woman living on the top floor
who had two sons, one a gangster and the other a cop,
her sorrow being that she didn't have a third to be a priest
and that way cover all possible professions;
and a German couple running the candy store downstairs,
who later go back to Germany with photographs of the
        neighborhood
and a complete list of the Jews there for the master file.

Life goes on, the good times and the bad:
Papa right away organizes the workers
and they go out on strike.
Little Sammy reads Tolstoy and Marx

17

and becomes a hothead radical and argues.
He goes around singing:

> *The hat workers' union*
> > *is a fascist union,*
> *The hat workers' union*
> > *is a fascist union,*
> *they preach socialism*
> > *but they practice fascism*
> *to make the world better for the boss class.*

At last George our hero is born, the fruit of freedom,
and settles down to his music lessons,
with the family standing around beaming
as he plays "Minuet in G."

Before long he is sneaking out of the house nights.
For crime? No. After girls? No,
he was playing piano for the silent films.
(What am I saying "films," nowadays they're films,
then they were movies.)

His father is furious when he learns about this:
George was only supposed to play religious music.
Sammy and Ethel were the secular wing of the family.
What was all this about jazz? That is music?
But playing organ in the synagogue one Friday night
George fell to dreaming and broke into ragtime,
and pretty soon all those old bearded Jews
are tapping their feet and smiling.
So George is kicked out into the hard world
with no blessing from his father except, "You bum you,"
and makes the rounds of Tin Pan Alley.

Sammy, the oldest, gives up Karl Marx
and marries a merchant's ugly daughter

and gets rich working in the business
and moves away to a better-class neighborhood like Brooklyn.

Little Ethel is growing up smart too,
and the struggling student who loves her
can hardly offer her the good times she had a right to
with her face and figure.
Pretty soon she is being driven home in a long limousine with
    curtains.
It pulled right up to the tenement door
with the neighbors staring from stoops and windows.
She drew a heavy veil over her face
and went up to the kitchen
where Ma turns a stone face to the stove.

"Look at you Ma," she says, "you're only forty.
I don't want that to happen to me,
so I'm getting out of this dump."
And she goes off to be kept by the Irish woman's gangster son,
who was making a million as a bootlegger.

George writes song hit after song hit
and meets Alexis Smith, a noble society woman with ice-blond
    hair,
who comes to his mother's house Friday nights
for the chicken soup and matzoh balls.
"You know Mother Bernstein, uptown we don't get food like
    this."
Anyway her French chef doesn't make it.
After about ten years' engagement
she gives George up because
she doesn't want to stand in the way of his music.

Meanwhile Ethel has been secretly putting her student
    through school
and paying the doctor bills for his crippled sister,

who wants to be a ballet dancer if the operation turns out
    successful.
But her gangster finally gets killed by his cop brother
when he comes, a fugitive, to his mother's kitchen door
and begs her to hide him from the law, and she says no.
He is then shot dead on the fire escape in the searchlights,
his blood dripping down on the elegant clothes
of Ethel weeping in the street below.

So Ethel comes back home and marries her student, now a
    lawyer,
but their first child is born dead
and the doctor says she will never be able to have another,
because of her past sins.

More success for George, in London and Paris,
command performance, cheering crowds, gray hair:
Tonight his great musical *Lower East Side* is opening
and it looks like a hit.
His leading lady loves him
but he always says, "As long as momma is alive . . ."

The curtain is about to go up on Act Three.
A telegram comes, his manager reads it:
PAPA HIT BY CAR, MOMMA HAS HEART ATTACK,
    COME AT ONCE. ETHEL.
The manager asks himself, Should I show it to him now?
George is standing in the wings ready to go out
and sing the finale himself.
His manager gives him the telegram.
He reads it as the orchestra plays the introduction, his cue.
The orchestra plays it again, and the audience starts
    murmuring.
George staggers out on stage humbly,
a small man with tears in his eyes,
holding the fatal telegram in his hand;
and looking up at the brightest light

20

that makes the tears click down his cheeks like diamonds,
he sings his big song.

Thunderous applause, cheers, rave reviews:
He takes the train to the funeral.
Standing around the grave, Ethel, Sammy, himself,
all grown up now, well dressed.
The old kitchen, oilcloth table top,
mama's pot she could always make soup in just by adding
    water.
What happened? Where did we go wrong?
Ethel and Sammy go away in their limousines:
"Got to be running along, kid. Call me sometime."
Alone. Mama, Papa, where are you?
Tears. A hand falls on his shoulder. His manager.
He looks long into the loving eyes. He decides.

He puts a coin in the pay phone: "Darling,
I want you to marry me, I love you."
He is calling his leading lady, who has long loved him.
"Oh George," she breathes, as the music
whirls up into a symphony of hearts full of happiness,
and the lovers rush into each other's arms in the middle of
    the stage
to sing the grand finale:
LOWER EAST SIDE.

The Bride of Frankenstein

The Baron has decided to mate the monster,
to breed him perhaps,
in the interests of pure science, his only god.

So he goes up into his laboratory
which he has built in the tower of the castle
to be as near the interplanetary forces as possible,
and puts together the prettiest monster-woman you ever saw
with a body like a pin-up girl
and hardly any stitching at all
where he sewed on the head of a raped and murdered beauty
    queen.

He sets his liquids burping, and coils blinking and buzzing,
and waits for an electric storm to send through the equipment
the spark vital for life.
The storm breaks over the castle
and the equipment really goes crazy
like a kitchen full of modern appliances
as the lightning juice starts oozing right into that pretty corpse.

He goes to get the monster
so he will be right there when she opens her eyes,
for she might fall in love with the first thing she sees as
    ducklings do.
That monster is already straining at his chains and slurping,
ready to go right to it:
He has been well prepared for coupling
by his pinching leering keeper who's been saying for weeks,
"Ya gonna get a little nookie, kid,"
or "How do you go for some poontang, baby?"
All the evil in him is focused on this one thing now
as he is led into her very presence.

She awakens slowly,
she bats her eyes,
she gets up out of the equipment,
and finally she stands in all her seamed glory,
a monster princess with a hairdo like a fright wig,
lightning flashing in the background
like a halo and a wedding veil,
like a photographer snapping pictures of great moments.

She stands and stares with her electric eyes,
beginning to understand that in this life too
she was just another body to be raped.

The monster is ready to go:
He roars with joy at the sight of her,
so they let him loose and he goes right for those knockers.
And she starts screaming to break your heart
and you realize that she was just born:
In spite of her big tits she was just a baby.

But her instincts are right—
rather death than that green slobber:
She jumps off the parapet.
And then the monster's sex drive goes wild.
Thwarted, it turns to violence, demonstrating sublimation
    crudely;
and he wrecks the lab, those burping acids and buzzing coils,
overturning the control panel so the equipment goes off like
    a bomb,
and the stone castle crumbles and crashes in the storm
destroying them all . . . perhaps.

Perhaps somehow the Baron got out of that wreckage of his
    dreams
with his evil intact, if not his good looks,
and more wicked than ever went on with his thrilling career.

And perhaps even the monster lived
to roam the earth, his desire still ungratified;
and lovers out walking in shadowy and deserted places
will see his shape loom up over them, their doom—
and children sleeping in their beds
will wake up in the dark night screaming
as his hideous body grabs them.

Sweet Gwendolyn and the Countess

The Countess rode out on her black horse in spring
wearing her black leather riding costume.
She was scouting for disciples in the countryside
and flicked with her whip the rosebuds as she passed.

Sweet Gwendolyn in her white dress
was out gathering May flowers.
Under sunshade hat, her pale face
blushed to the singing bees,
and her golden curls lay passive on bent shoulders
as she stooped to pluck a white lily.

The Countess passing by took one look,
galloped up, and reined her stallion sharply in,
high over the modest figure
of Sweet Gwendolyn with the downcast eyes.
She leaped down from her horse and knelt,
laying the whip in tribute before the golden girl.

That foolish one swooned forward to the ground
in a great white puff of dress fabric
and a scattering of flowers. At that,
the Countess rose in all her black pride
and put her dirty leather boot hard on Gwendolyn's bent neck,
pushing down the golden head to the grass,
and gave her a smart lash across her innocently upturned
    behind.

Gwendolyn looked up with begging eyes
and a small whimper of submission,
as the Countess pushed her over and threw the skirt up,
exposing legs and bottom bare,

and shoved the leather whip handle between squeezed thighs
    of virtue
forcing them apart to reveal the pink pulsing maidenhood.

Poor Gwendolyn moaned with shame and pain
as she lay back crushing her Mayflowers, exposed and
    unresisting—
until the Countess, in full charge, pulled her to her feet,
tied the whip end around her neck,
remounted the big black horse
and slowly trotted off,
leading the sobbing girl a captive behind her
off to her dark castle.

The Life of Joan Crawford

For Barbara Barry

She was a working girl from a small town
but the town wasn't so small
that it didn't have a railroad track
dividing the right side from the wrong side.
On the right side was the Hill
where the swells lived in big houses,
and on the wrong side, the Hollow where the proletariat
spent their greasy and unrewarding lives.
(For in those days the American town
was a living demonstration of Marxist theory.)

Joan of course lived in the Hollow
in one of those shacks with sagging porches
the mill put up rows of for the workers.
Her father, Tim Crawford, was the town drunk
living on relief and odd jobs
ever since the mines closed down when Joan was a baby.
He had been waiting for them to reopen for twenty years.
Joan never knew what had happened to her mother:
Joan's birth, her mother's disappearance or death, the mine's
    closing,
that was in a time of violence no one would discuss.
Just mention it and her father went on a binge,
not that he was ever sober.

She sighed, and went off to work in the five-and-ten
wearing her made-over dress with little washable collar and
    cuffs.
Even with her prole accent and the cheap bag and shoes
she was a good looker.
Men used to come by in their flashy suits and big cigars,
call her tootsie and ask for a date,

but she knew a poor girl didn't stand a chance with them.
She wasn't one of those innocents
who think a guy loves you if he gets a hard-on.
Yet she wouldn't go with any of the boys from the Hollow
because with them the future was sleazy with kids
and the ruin of her figure before she was thirty—
and no fun after the honeymoon
except the Friday-night fight
when he would come home stinking, having drunk up the
    paycheck
and beat her black and blue
when she threw the stack of overdue bills at him
and then screw her viciously on the dining-room table.
Some fun.
That was life in the Hollow and she wasn't having any.
She had turned down a job working in the mill
where the pay was better but life closed like a trap on you
and chose the more ladylike job at the five-and-ten
where people called her Miss and she could pose genteelly
behind the Tangee cosmetic display and the ribbon counter.
For Joan had the makings of a lady
if she could ever get some dough to fix herself up with
and a speech teacher to correct her dreadful accent.

But Nature had its way with Joan at last:
Spring came and handsome John Wainrich
(of the best family in town—they owned everything,
the five-and-dime, the shut mines, and the mill),
John Wainrich came in one day to collect the receipts or
    something
and found a million dollar baby in his own five and ten
    cents store.
Well Joan fell hard
and went out with him in his big car
and of course in the moonlight she let him have his way
    with her.
She used to meet him on the sly

when he could get away from the country club
and the milk-white debutante he was engaged to,
and they would drive out to roadhouses
where he wouldn't be seen by his swell friends.
Joan had pride,
but what is a woman's pride when she's in love.
What it came to, a few months later,
was that she got pregnant,
and just as she was about to break the good news,
he told her he was going to be married
and would have to stop seeing her until after the wedding,
that it was just a marriage of convenience
and wouldn't make any difference to them.
So she couldn't tell him then, she would have died first.

My great love, she muttered sarcastically,
he didn't even use a scum-bag.
And she went off to the city
where she got a job as receptionist in an office.
Her boss, Mr. Harris, was an older but dignified man
with a wife at home on Park Avenue, the victim of neurosis
    and wealth—
with all that money she could buy neither health nor
    happiness.
Joan used to listen to Mr. Harris's troubles
when she brought him his alka-seltzer mornings.
And when she was promoted to secretary, they would have
    dinner out
and she'd advise him on business,
she being a girl with a good head on her shoulders.

In Mr. Harris's company she saw the world and learned fast.
She lost her small-town look and learned to dress,
wearing hat and gloves, to fluff out her hair
and drink vermouth cocktails.
And while retaining the colorful idiom of the Hollow,
her grammar improved and her voice lost its nasal whine.

Joan was a knockout in every way
from honest eyes and square shoulders
to the narrow hips of a tango dancer.

Nothing showed yet in the baby department.
At night Joan looked critically at herself in the mirror:
Not a bulge, but baby was in there all right,
and her eyes went bitter as she thought of its father—
her great love, hmph.
"Well young feller, at least we'll have each other.
But I'd better be making preparations.
A working girl can't leave things to the caterer."

Then her boss proposed: He'd divorce his wife and marry her.
"Gee Mr. Harris, I think you're swell but I can't.
There is a real big favor you could do for me, though,"
and she told him how she gave her all for love
and her lover turned out to be a louse.
So Mr. Harris set her up in a little flat until the baby came.
He didn't make any demands on her or anything,
not yet anyway: It was sort of a promissory note
to be paid off later when she grew to love him out of
     gratitude.

But her ex-lover, John Wainrich, came to town
with his new wedding ring on, and tracked her down;
and misunderstanding the arrangement, called her a few
     names,
but swore she was his and he'd never give her up.
Joan still loved him but had the courage
to flee to a cheap hotel.
She got a job as dance-hall hostess, dime-a-dance,
six months pregnant, but with a brave smile
as the customers stepped on her toes.
They found her a good joe and a willing ear
as they told her their troubles
while rubbing off against her to a slow foxtrot.

One of her customers, impressed by her dancing,
got her to enter a dance marathon with him for prize money—
she needed that dough for the little stranger—
but the strain was too much for her,
marathon-dancing in her seventh month!

She came to on a hospital bed
with no makeup on and a white cloth over her forehead like
    a nun
to see her griddle-faced father looking down on her,
his mouth boozy as ever, but in his heart
vowing to go on the wagon if God would spare her life:
"Come home with me, Joanie, I'll take care of you."
"And baby too, papa?"
"Didn't they tell you, Joanie? The baby . . ."
"Oh no . . ."
And tears of mourning still in her eyes
she went back home to the Hollow and kept house for her
    father.

She had two visits shortly after returning home:
First, John's pale bride came by, big with child,
neglect driving her to seek out her rival.
When she saw Joan so sweet and good
instead of some tramp homewrecker type,
she burst into tears and confessed she knew John didn't
    love her
but hoped he would when the baby was born, his heir.
The bitterness in Joan's heart turned to pity—
weren't they both women who had suffered?—
so she forgave her and they wept together:
Joan never could resist being a pal.

The other visit was from old Mr. Wainrich, John's father.
(Never had the Hollow seen so many long cars drive
    through.)
The old capitalist had a confession to make:

"When I saw you at the window watering the geraniums
I could have sworn you were your mother."
"You knew my mother, Mr. Wainrich?" asked Joan astonished.
"Yes. Bette wasn't like the other women in the Hollow.
She was a Davis you know. Her parents
had been plantation people down in Georgia
and even if they did end up here in the Hollow
she never forgot that she was a thoroughbred."
"Are you trying to tell me that you loved my mother?" Joan
gasped.

"Yes, I loved her, but the heir to an industrial empire
isn't free to marry whom he chooses,
so my family chose an appropriate bride for me.
At that time I was running our coal mines here,
where Tim Crawford worked.
He was the biggest and toughest man in the Hollow
so naturally he was spokesman for the boys.
He had loved your mother for years
but she knew what it meant for a woman to marry a miner
and live in constant fear of a cave-in.
And she hated his coarse language and crude manners: she
was a lady.
And besides, she loved me.
But when I broke the news of my engagement to her
(I explained it was just a marriage of convenience
and it wouldn't make any difference to us)
she married Tim just to spite me.
But it wasn't enough for her: right on my wedding day
she got Tim Crawford to call the men out on strike,
and, with violence surging around the Hill,
I had the biggest wedding ever seen in these parts.
I was coal and my bride was steel: what a merger!
The President came, and there were reporters from Chicago,
and your mother, already big with child, leading a picket
line.

32

That strike went on for months, and you were born in the
middle of it.
But we couldn't go on apart, your mother and I.
We knew we were sinners, but we managed to meet on the
sly,
although the strike had turned the town into a battlefield
and we belonged to opposing armies.
Finally we decided to run away together, but just at that
time
a load of scabs I was importing to work the mines arrived,
and there was a tremendous battle between them and the
miners,
led by Tim Crawford of course.
The miners had lead pipes and dynamite,
but we had the National Guard in full battle dress.
Your mother and I, eloping, got caught in the middle
and took refuge in a deserted mine;
and I don't know which side did it, but a stick of dynamite
was thrown down the shaft, and your mother
was buried by a ton of falling rock."
(Joan moaned and hid her face in her hands.)
"It was useless to do anything so I left her there.
Why say anything when no one knew?
She was destroyed by the strike she had started.
The mines were shut down for good of course,
I couldn't bear the memory.
They would have had to be shut anyway,
we were losing money on them."
"And that's why daddy never knew what happened to mother,
raising me all by himself, and took to drink . . ."
"Yes, and I went back home to my wife and our little John
was born
and I tried to forget . . ."
"Promise me one thing, Mr. Wainrich," Joan said,
"for the sake of my mother's memory,
that you'll open the mines again and give daddy back his
old job."

33

Joan had a lot to think about in the days that followed.
One day she got a call to come up right away to the big
    house,
and arriving, found John's wife dying,
having given birth to a child, and asking for her.
The pale bride lay holding her child, the Wainrich heir,
but seeing Joan, she sat up with her last strength and said,
"I give him to you," and fell back dead.
Joan fainted away, and when she came to,
it seemed a long time later, after the funeral and the
    mourning,
John Wainrich held her in his arms and was saying over and
    over,
"I am yours now, she gave me to you."
"But she meant the child," Joan cried.
"Both of us are yours, my darling."

So Joan found her place in life at last.
They always said she'd make it up there, surrounded by the
    help,
a lady, moving gracefully among the guests.
And what a difference now:
The miners in tuxes standing around the punchbowl with the
    swells,
the colored butler joining in the fun with loud yaks,
a new era, the classless society,
brought about by the smartest little woman in the U.S.A.,
Ladies and Gentlemen: Miss Joan Crawford.

Whatever Happened to May Caspar?

A Narration for an Animated Cartoon

What happens to old movie stars,
those faded queens of stage and screen?
They move into hotels off Times Square maybe
where they live among their souvenirs,
near the lights, the people, the premières
that no longer know them—
funny old ladies with hair a pink frizz,
salvaging old costumes for street clothes.

Does anyone remember May Caspar now?
She was all the rage in thirty-three
when she starred in *May Morning* with Ronald Peale,
in which she played a simple country girl
and he a prince who lost his heart among the apple blossoms.

Now thirty years later (that makes her about sixty, at least),
what does she see when she sits down to her vanity table
with its clutter of lotions?
Does she stare at the blur in the mirror
and remember how young she was in that movie,
how pure and fragile?
Before she puts on her glasses
she takes a swig out of a large perfume bottle,
and goes about painting a kewpie doll over the wreck of her
    face:
Somehow it always comes out crooked.

Later, after her disastrous marriage to Nick Kinsella
and the divorce and the operations
(they say he beat her up horribly),
after she got back her looks,
she played *femme fatale* roles on divans with heavy eye
    makeup.

Remember *A Woman's Eyes,* with Ivan Carlovan,
in which May was the toast of Vienna
until the love of her prince turned to hate
when he discovered a stableboy was her lover
and she had to flee through snowdrifts in a sleigh
standing up behind the horses singing:
>   *The heart will find a way*
but ending up in a waterfront bar in Marseilles
singing with an accordion:
>   *A woman's eyes are pools of sin.*
>   *Don't look too long, they'll lure you in.*
There were dozens of suicides to her record of that song.

Then came her greatest hit, *The Downward Path,*
in which she played a mature stage star
who fell in love with a young actor,
but he only used her to make it to the top
while she went downhill fast and ended in the gutter
selling flowers by the stage door
as he came out with the ingénue on his arm,
and stepped into the waiting limousine.
How her beautiful eyes shone in that scene!
You knew she held no grudge, but loved him still
as she sang after him:
>   *Go, beautiful youth,*
>   *forget me now, for I am old.*
>   *Enjoy your fame as I did mine.*
For that, America forgave her everything,
her parade of unsuitable husbands,
her drunken brawls in restaurants.
She was darling May Caspar, for a few years anyway
(her career lasted only three more years),
then she faded away.

Now forgotten, she is that funny old lady
living shabbily on a dwindling income
in a Times Square hotel, once genteel,

now full of call girls and Kansas tourists.
It gets harder and harder to pay the bills.
Back rent mounts up. Room service is cut off.
She lives on hot dogs. Her fate looks grim.
She is about to be put out in the street
with her souvenirs and wardrobe
for the winter wind to blow away,
plumes and bits of fur and photographs and dried corsages,
and she skittering after them down the streets.

But wait, here comes a late rider:
A message from the Museum of Modern Art!
They are planning a May Caspar revival
and she is wanted to appear "in person," like the old days.
May Caspar movies stamped Authentic American Art.
She is proclaimed A Great Actress.
May Caspar Called Back to Hollywood to Make Film.
But first she goes to Last Chance,
exclusive beauty resort in Death Valley,
where they go to work on her
with hormones, vitamins, embryo implants, and surgery.

When she shows up in Hollywood her beauty is restored.
Thirty years of ravagement have been erased:
There is not a wrinkle.
Of course her strength is not what it was—
two men have to hold her up,
but she is a great trouper and the show will go on.
Today they are filming her big scene on the divan, her
    trademark:
Lights, Camera, Action: May Caspar acts again!

Anyway she tries, but the effort is too much for her—
the hot lights, the excitement,
her skin held taut by invisible clips,
her heart stimulated with drugs,
her head sweating under the wig,

every bit of her is held together with string and sealing wax.
"Okay Miss Caspar, give it all you've got."
The camera moves in inexorably for the closeup.
She tries desperately to think young, to hold everything up.
Those merciless lights!
Too late, it all collapses.

Goodbye May Caspar.
We loved you
in the way we love—
faithlessly.
Or are we, growing older,
ready to remember again
our great loves
of yesteryear
and go search for them
where we lost sight of them
in those shabby places,
close to the brightest
lights
that cast the deepest
shadow?

The Return of Frankenstein

He didn't die in the whirlpool by the mill
where he had fallen in after a wild chase
by all the people of the town.

Somehow he clung to an overhanging rock
until the villagers went away.

And when he came out, he was changed forever,
that soft heart of his had hardened
and he really was a monster now.

He was out to pay them back,
to throw the lie of brotherly love
in their white Christian teeth.

Wasn't his flesh human flesh
even made from the bodies of criminals,
the worst the Baron could find?

But love is not necessarily implicit in human flesh:
Their hatred was now his hatred,

so he set out on his new career
his previous one being the victim,
the good man who suffers.

Now no longer the hunted but the hunter
he was in charge of his destiny
and knew how to be cold and clever,

preserving barely a spark of memory
for the old blind musician
who once took him in and offered brotherhood.

39

His idea—if his career now had an idea—
was to kill them all,
keep them in terror anyway,
let them feel hunted.
Then perhaps they would look at others
with a little pity and love.

Only a suffering people have any virtue.

White Jungle Queen

What a girl I was, going in, all innocence,
into the jungle with my father, Dr. Weatherbun.
We were out to explore
the last remaining jungle in All Africa
now that everything else there is like Havana or New York.

But when we arrived
at the edge of the unknown world
of tribes and their gods
the bearers we got from the Real Native Employment Agency
dropped their bales and fled.
"No go there sahib. Bad spirit live there."

I didn't blame them really—
how do people live in such a scary world?
And I thought of my nice lunchcounter job
in Kissin' Trees, Carolina, and daddy,
that's Dr. Witherspoon, going off every day
to his university job, until the Ford Foundation
gave him this grant; it just shows you
what you can get nowadays if you fill in the application!

Well, without the porters
we had to leave behind all our comforts.
I'd hoped we could sit in armchairs
dressed in cool summer frocks sipping drinks
and watch the natives dancing around the fire.

So we stepped across the magic line
that separates the known from the unknown
where the hungry things live. The very word hungry
sounds like a drooling mouth chomping away at you,
and there the gods are always hungry
and the tribes have to keep feeding them like servants.

So when people look at you, they see a roast turkey on a
    plate:
You are money to them, kind of a currency
they can use to buy something else.

We no sooner stepped into the jungle, the tom-toms started
and we were surrounded, and seized:
Those people paint themselves with eyes all over
so you don't know where to look for the real eyes
and you look at the painted eyes and want to beg them
to spare you, to love you, to stop
thinking what they're thinking! You're good, you really are,
and you would love them if you got the chance
even black as they are,
and me a girl from the South!

So we disappeared into the world beyond sun,
into a nightworld, where laws of sleep run things
and dreams live. I wanted to let go, let go,
and sink into a deeper sleep where the dreaming would stop
but they carried us on to what a girl like me
was never meant to know.
I was only ninety-eight pounds of American teen-ager
when I went with my father, Professor Weymouth
on a scientific expedition to explore a jungle.

I'll skip the details of how they took us to their village
and put us in a grass hut—it's exactly like you've seen in the
    movies.
What happened later was that we got away
by breaking through the wall of the hut,
and ran into the jungle;
and the wild beasts came after us like quarry.
They must have got daddy
because I heard somewhere behind me his scream and the
    growls

and then the grunting of eating and his groans,
and I couldn't listen anymore, I just ran.

I was frantic to get out of the forest:.
I could see myself breaking through into the surrounding
    fields
and heading straight for the port, and staggering home,
and settling down with a good man for life
in Kissin' Trees, Carolina. But it wasn't to be.
I ran until I couldn't run anymore
and my fear led me in circles back to the village.
I think the savages were even watching
and keeping the wild beasts off.
They knew what they wanted, a sacrifice for their gods,
or in their language: *Karpissu por Kong.*

That night they tied me blonde and naked to a stake
piled up with faggots
and started dancing around me to the tom-toms:
You can imagine all of them big and shiny with those spears!
It was like the KKK was suddenly all Negroes
and they were in a position to make me pay
for everything awful that had been done them;
and how I would have made up to them for all that if I could,
but not by being burned alive! Any other way!
Suddenly they seized flaming branches
and threw them on the fuel piled around me
and I prayed and prayed and prayed
as the flames ate their way towards me . . .
and you know what? There was a crash of thunder
and that show was totally rained out!

Well, the gods had spoken
so they untied me, and laid me swooning on a lion skin,
and made me queen.

The strange thing was I felt the power come over me then,
and their gods were my gods
and I was their white queen in a leopard skin bikini:
Does every southern white girl dream of this?
So of course I stayed: This is my life now.
However, when they do the movie version of my story
I think Elizabeth Taylor should play me, don't you?
I see her in a blond wig with hair tumbling to her knees.
I'm writing the screenplay myself.

Can't you just see me at the world première in Hollywood
in my leopard skin nothings and marching behind me
my tall tribe of warriors, every one of them a beauty?
That's my only dream.
Anyway, until then I'm not in any pain,
if you get what I mean, honey.
(Akimba darling, get me another mango.)
All I have to do is lie back and wait for Hollywood to call.

Nancy

When scolded by Aunt Fritzy Ritz
Nancy seems to lose her wits.
Nancy is very often cross
but Fritzy's the undisputed boss.
She sits in the house reading the papers
supervising Nancy's capers.

Aunt Fritzy's a peculiar sort:
She has no visible means of support.
She never seems to earn a bean
and there's no "uncle" on the scene.
The questions seem to rise a lot:
Is Fritzy Nancy's aunt, or not?
If Fritzy is related to
that awful Mrs. Meany who
Annie Roonie had to flee,
then who can Nancy really be?

Rumors are flying thick and fast;
stories from mouth to ear are passed:
"Who is Fritzy Ritz indeed
but someone overcome by greed.
Welfare pays a monthly sum
to keep that orphan in her home.
Although she looks like Etta Kett
She's older, more depraved, in debt."

One scandalous version I have heard
(of which I don't believe a word)
says Nancy's father, coming back
a little early from the track,
found his wife and Fritzy in
a most revolting act of sin.
With a knife he tried to nip

45

this lesbian relationship:
Saw red, and stabbed; the blow went wild
and made an orphan of his child.
His wife was dead, he got the chair,
the court named Fritzy Ritz as heir.
The child, the house, the bank account,
were left to Fritzy Ritz, the "aunt."

No one will make Aunt Fritzy crawl
now that she's in charge of all:
the house, the grounds, the little brat.
She'll teach her to remember that!

Poor Nancy's nature has been bent
by this negative environment.
She never will grow up at all
but stay forever three feet tall.

PART TWO:

SELECTED SHORT SUBJECTS

To Ganapati, Hindu God of Auspiciousness

A domestic god seems to be running things lately
and the gods of public life, glamor, and art
have gone on to those who want them.

Mine is the god of golden hands, four of them,
who sets me to fixing, building, cooking, and cleaning.
I cut hair, serve meals, grow plants, sew pants.

The plants smile at me while drying up from steam heat,
the food sings to me from the frying pan,
the chair I repair trembles and sighs.

I have served under other gods:
The baboon made me universal sex slave
and under the crocodile I made the literary scene.
With the Roarer, lion god, I tried to save the world.

Now I only pray to Ganapati
with his friendly elephant's head, humor in his eyes,
and four hands to deal lucky cards with.

But I see a time coming, and soon,
when I have to get a job unless you, dear elephant,
save me by fiddling with my horoscope.
Do you see a Ford fellowship in my future?

Well, I will pray for that divine aid when I must.
Now the radiators are puffing
and I can sit at my desk near the bed
spread with the colors of Morocco.

There's plenty of time later for ambition
or if not, so what, I don't feel like it anyway.
May these auspicious times continue, Ganapati,
just keep the wolf from my door.

Both My Grandmothers

I. My Polish Grandma

Grandma and the children left at night.
It was forbidden to go. In those days
the Czar and his cossacks rode through the town at whim
killing Jews and setting fire to straw roofs
while just down the road the local Poles
sat laughing as they drank liquor.

Grandpa had gone to America first
and earned the money for the rest of the family to come over.
So they left finally, the whole brood of them
with the hired agent running the show,
an impatient man, and there were so many kids
and the bundles kept falling apart
and poor grandma was frightened of him.

She gave the man all the money
but she couldn't round up the kids fast enough for him.
They were children after all and didn't understand
and she was so stupid and clumsy herself,
carrying food for all of them and their clothes
and could she leave behind her pots?
Her legs hurt already; they were always swollen
from the hard work, the childbearing, and the cold.

They caught the train and there was a terrible moment
when the conductor came by for the tickets:
The children mustn't speak or he would know they were Jewish,
they had no permits to travel—Jews weren't allowed.
But the agent knew how to handle it,
everybody got *shmeared*, that means money got you
  everywhere.

The border was the worst. They had to sneak across at night.

The children mustn't make a sound, not even the babies.
Momma was six and she didn't want to do anything wrong
but she wasn't sure what to do.
The man led them through the woods
and beyond they could hear dogs barking from the sentry hut,
and then they had to run all of them down the ravine to the
	other side,
grandma broken down from childbearing with her bundles
and bad legs and a baby in her arms,
they ran all the children across the border
or the guards might shoot them
and if the little ones cried, the agent said he would smother
	them.

They got to a port finally.
Grandpa had arranged for cabin passage, not steerage,
but the agent cheated and put them in the hold
so they were on the low deck looking up at the rich people.
My momma told me how grandma took care of all her children,
how Jake didn't move anymore he was so seasick, maybe even
	dead,
and if people thought he was dead
they would throw him overboard like garbage, so she hid him.
The rich tossed down oranges to the poor children—
my momma had never had one before.

They came to New York, to the tenements,
a fearful new place, a city, country people in the city.
My momma, who had been roly-poly in slow Poland,
got skinny and pimply in zippy New York.
Everybody grew up in a new way.
And now my grandma is dead and my momma is old
and we her children are all scattered over the earth
speaking a different language and forgetting
why it was so important
to go to a new country.

51

II. My Russian Grandma

When my father's father went to America
to earn the money for the family to come over later
my grandma had to take care of all six kids alone.

One day coming home from market,
with a baby in one arm and a bag of potatoes in the other,
she was crossing the tracks not paying attention
when she saw the train coming right up on her.
She jumped, dropping potatoes and baby on the tracks
as the train passed over
cutting the child to pieces; and in her grief
she reached under the turning wheels
to pick up the pieces of her baby
and got half her fingers cut off
and a bang on the head that knocked her cold.

Strangers took her to the hospital
where she came to, not knowing who she was or where she
      was—
it was a blessing for her to forget for a while.

But meanwhile the children were left alone.
When their mama didn't come
they huddled in the house afraid and crying,
except my father who went out to beg for food.
He kept them alive for all those terrible months.

And when grandma finally came home from the hospital
with her hands bandaged and anyway useless now
she found them all covered with lice and filthy,
and got to work like a whirlwind
to clean them up as best she could.
But it was too late: the hunger had weakened them
and the lice brought the fever,
and they all died but my father and one girl.

Then with the house half-empty
and in her bitterness and sorrow
my grandma took a lover—who could blame her
for needing a man at such a time?
Perhaps at first he was just a boarder
she took in to help with expenses.
But my father who had taken charge of the family
hated him and tried to throw him out
the way little boys do, so the man beat him,
and my father took to cowering behind the furniture
living such a life of horror and fear
that he still stammers from it.

The money came from America eventually
and grandma and her two remaining children left Russia
    forever.
She would die in the new land of an earache,
my grandma who put sugar in my father's soup to fatten him
    up—
if he got fat she would know he was consoled.

My sister Barbara, being the first girl
born after grandma's death,
should have been named Marsha after her,
according to our traditions
of reincarnating the dead in the living
(as I should have been called Abraham
after my great-grandfather, now unknown to me forever).

Historians aren't writing our histories
so it is up to us to do it for ourselves,
but I know so little: this legend and her name.

Well, before everything is finally lost to us all
I write this remnant down.

Daisy

Daisy is my horse's name.
She's small for a horse and piebald
like those the Indians ride bareback in the movies.

We'll set out overland, she and I,
for the great Pacific Northwest,
a wild land of lakes and forests to wander in.

Come blizzard in the high meadows,
I'll get off and lead her,
our heads low in the driving snow, looking for shelter,

a windbreak of pines or maybe a leaning rock.
And as Daisy dozes steamily overhead,
I'll roll up in my blanket at her feet and go to sleep

until a velvet mouth wakes me
to a big brown horsy eye
and a clear morning in the snowfields.

The Death of Clyde Beatty

d. July 20, 1965

1

Oh no, he didn't die of cancer,
don't tell me that,
not Clyde Beatty who tamed lions and tigers.

Clyde Beatty died in the ring
clawed to death by Old Ugly, half-lion, half-tiger,
the tiglon nobody could tame.

That Old Devil got him
because an animal like that won't play the circus game
where man is supposed to win out over fate.

They warned Clyde Beatty that this one was a killer
but that was the kind of challenge he loved,
so he put on his superman suit
and went into the cage with the animals,
shot off his blanks, cracked his whip,
and jockeyed them with his chair
into position on the pedestals,
a classroom of good little lions and tigers
while teacher turns his back
and takes a bow.

That was when Old Killer got him,
when he turned away to bow,
and even though we shouted, No! No!
we were on the side of Mr. Green Eyes
as he jumped from his silly stool
broke the little whip with a bite,
and with a swipe of paw smashed the chair
and grabbed a tiny Clyde Beatty like a doll
in his striped and toothy grin,

and that was the end of him
on the sawdust
with the band thumping away
to cover the disaster with a cheery noise.

2

Yes, from cancer . . . but however it was,
it was Mr. Death who ate him up alive
as he does us all one way or another.
One day he introduces himself:
You Clyde, Me Death; let's go, beautiful.
We are truly married to adventure.

Lion tamers, come on home.
Why should beasts sit still
to a man's orders?
What does that prove anymore?

For no matter how many of them you tamed, Clyde Beatty,
there was still one that stalked your jungles,
that went on a rampage down your valleys
(where your natives shivered in flimsy huts
listening to screams in the night),
a mystery beast who was only satisfied finally
with your entire body and soul.

We call him cancer but he is unnameable.
Doctors inject you with poison, but can't kill him.
They cut you up but can't cut him out.
He eats you away like a secret,
maybe your own secret that you never let yourself in on.

I'd rather Clyde Beatty died in the ring
with his combat boots on,
but anyway, he's off now in the special heaven

for those who choose to go into the lion's den
and risk their lives facing the big beasts for us all:
He's up there with Frank Buck, Martin and Osa Johnson,
Hemingway, Tarzan, and Bomba,
where he belongs.

Playing in the Back Fields

All the kids on the block, Sonny, Totsy, me and my sisters,
used to gather under the sumac bushes in the back fields,
and sitting in a circle, pull down pants and bloomers,
and stare and stare at each other:
We called it dirty stuff.

In the row of houses above us
mothers would look out of upstairs windows from time to
　　　time
to see the children were all right.
We never could imagine that the thin sumac branches
did not shield us from our anxious mothers' eyes.

When they saw us in the magic circle with our pants down
their screams of "Come in this minute" rang out,
and we knew we were caught again doing the Most
　　　Forbidden,
and ran home, already crying,
before we got the spanking of our lives.

Plant Poems

1

As the leading agronomist   in the Kharkov Agricultural
                               Institute
I want to announce the discovery   that plants feel as we do
but since they cannot talk   they are considered insensible.

Actually they do make sounds
but on a different wavelength   than our ears can hear
and when you chop up a lettuce   it is saying Ouch.

2

I once had a plant on my windowsill
that grew down the outside of the building in summer.
It was all leaves at my end where I watered it
(that plant drank tons of water),
but visiting the people in the apartment below one day
I saw it blooming in their window.

3

When I bring water into the room
the plants start sending out
tremors of excitement
that water produces on their senses.

Like your cat rubs against your legs
talking out loud
while you open the can of catfood.

59

My apartment is shabby really
but especially at night in lamplight it glows.
It's the plants that do that.

Plants are beings of great richness.
Of course they must be tended faithfully like pets
or like a monster child that will never grow up
but stay home with you always
and have to be fed and looked after.

I never understand the tragedy of an idiot child:
People don't mind having a dog around the house to love.
Well that kind of child is the same thing.
It doesn't go to school or on dates or get a job.
That is no more in its nature
than for plants to bark or make a mess
(bless you, green ones, for that)
but what a glow they bring to every room.

World War II

It was over Target Berlin the flak shot up our plane
just as we were dumping bombs on the already smoking city
on signal from the lead bomber in the squadron.
The plane jumped again and again as the shells burst under us
sending jagged pieces of steel rattling through our fuselage.
I'll never understand
how none of us got ripped by those fragments.

Then, being hit, we had to drop out of formation right away
losing speed and altitude,
and when I figured out our course with trembling hands
  on the instruments
(I was navigator)
we set out on the long trip home to England
alone, with two of our four engines gone
and gas streaming out of holes in the wing tanks.
That morning at briefing
we had been warned not to go to nearby Poland
partly liberated then by the Russians,
although later we learned that another crew in trouble
had landed there anyway,
and patching up their plane somehow,
returned gradually to England
roundabout by way of Turkey and North Africa.
But we chose England, and luckily
the Germans had no fighters to send up after us then
for this was just before they developed their jet.
To lighten our load we threw out
guns and ammunition, my navigation books, all the junk
and made it over Holland
with a few goodbye fireworks from the shore guns.

Over the North Sea the third engine gave out
and we dropped low over the water.

The gas gauge read empty but by keeping the nose down
a little gas at the bottom of the tank sloshed forward
and kept our single engine going.
High overhead, the squadrons were flying home in formation
—the raids had gone on for hours after us.
Did they see us down there in our trouble?
We radioed our final position for help to come
but had no idea if anyone
happened to be tuned in and heard us,
and we crouched together on the floor
knees drawn up and head down
in regulation position for ditching;
listened as the engine stopped, a terrible silence,
and we went down into the sea with a crash,
just like hitting a brick wall,
jarring bones, teeth, eyeballs panicky.
Who would ever think water could be so hard?
You black out, and then come to
with water rushing in like a sinking-ship movie.

All ten of us started getting out of there fast:
There was a convenient door in the roof to climb out by,
one at a time. We stood in line,
water up to our thighs and rising.
The plane was supposed to float for twenty seconds
but with all those flak holes
who could say how long it really would?
The two life rafts popped out of the sides into the water
but one of them only half inflated
and the other couldn't hold everyone
although they all piled into it, except the pilot,
who got into the limp raft that just floated.
The radio operator and I, out last,
(Did that mean we were least aggressive, least likely to
       survive?)
we stood on the wing watching the two rafts

being swept off by waves in different directions.
We had to swim for it.
Later they said the cords holding rafts to plane
broke by themselves, but I wouldn't have blamed them
for cutting them loose, for fear
that by waiting the plane would go down
and drag them with it.

I headed for the overcrowded good raft
and after a clumsy swim in soaked heavy flying clothes
got there and hung onto the side.
The radio operator went for the half-inflated raft
where the pilot lay with water sloshing over him,
but he couldn't swim, even with his life vest on,
being from the Great Plains—
his strong farmer's body didn't know
how to wallow through the water properly
and a wild current seemed to sweep him farther off.
One minute we saw him on top of a swell
and perhaps we glanced away for a minute
but when we looked again he was gone—
just as the plane went down sometime around then
when nobody was looking.

It was midwinter and the waves were mountains
and the water ice water.
You could live in it twenty-five minutes
the Ditching Survival Manual said.
Since most of the crew were squeezed on my raft
I had to stay in the water hanging on.
My raft? It was their raft, they got there first so they would live.
Twenty-five minutes I had.
Live, live, I said to myself.
You've got to live.
There looked like plenty of room on the raft
from where I was and I said so

but they said no.
When I figured the twenty-five minutes were about up
and I was getting numb,
I said I couldn't hold on anymore,
and a little rat-faced boy from Alabama, one of the gunners,
got into the icy water in my place,
and I got on the raft in his.
He insisted on taking off his flying clothes
which was probably his downfall because even wet clothes
      are protection,
and then worked hard, kicking with his legs, and we all
      paddled,
to get to the other raft,
and we tied them together.
The gunner got in the raft with the pilot
and lay in the wet.
Shortly after, the pilot started gurgling green foam from his
      mouth—
maybe he was injured in the crash against the instruments—
and by the time we were rescued,
he and the little gunner were both dead.

That boy who took my place in the water
who died instead of me
I don't remember his name even.
It was like those who survived the death camps
by letting others go into the ovens in their place.
It was him or me, and I made up my mind to live.
I'm a good swimmer,
but I didn't swim off in that scary sea
looking for the radio operator when he was washed away.
I suppose, then, once and for all,
I chose to live rather than be a hero, as I still do today,
although at that time I believed in being heroic, in saving
      the world,
even if, when opportunity knocked,
I instinctively chose survival.

As evening fell the waves calmed down
and we spotted a boat, far off, and signaled with a flare gun,
hoping it was English not German.
The only two who cried on being found
were me and a boy from Boston, a gunner.
The rest of the crew kept straight faces.

It was a British air-sea rescue boat:
They hoisted us up on deck,
dried off the living and gave us whisky and put us to bed,
and rolled the dead up in blankets,
and delivered us all to a hospital on shore
for treatment or disposal.
None of us even caught cold, only the dead.

This was a minor accident of war:
Two weeks in a rest camp at Southport on the Irish Sea
and we were back at Grafton-Underwood, our base,
ready for combat again,
the dead crewmen replaced by living ones,
and went on hauling bombs over the continent of Europe,
destroying the Germans and their cities.

It

When her breasts started growing
she bound them down with a strap.
She was ashamed to have them stick out
so people could tease her—
even if she had always looked forward to having them
and stared at the brassiere ads.

It's harder (so to speak) for boys.
Suddenly it is sticking out in front of you
what nobody had ever mentioned,
and even a jockstrap doesn't help much.
And even worse, maybe, is the come.
What do you do with the stuff when it spurts out?

My mother always said how important it was
to prepare girls for what was about to happen
so they shouldn't pick up wrong ideas
from other girls like she did,
or think they were dying
when they woke up one day in a pool of blood.

I was always listening while she taught my sisters
what to expect from nature and to say no until marriage.
Of girls you could speak; boys were unmentionable.
She must have believed about boys
that if you train them not to touch it
and don't ever mention it, it doesn't exist.

But it did: I woke up one morning
with a hard-on that wouldn't go down,
come all over the sheets and no way to wipe it up
and the whole family around and nowhere to hide.
This was unthinkable, and I prayed and prayed
for it to go away forever.

And the terrible act I couldn't help doing although I vowed
    to stop
and half-losing consciousness in the pleasure:
How to remember to think of the gooey mess, and watch out?
Does it show? Can they smell it? Did I make any noise?
You must control yourself, I ordered desperately,
or your life will be ruined like it says in the handbook.

I couldn't control it nor did it go away:
Too bad there wasn't the horrible exposure I dreaded
because as it was I kept it secret—
I was alone in the whole world with it,
and while trying to destroy it, I almost destroyed myself.
Only now, after years of struggle,
I face the simple facts of nature
and think how useless to have suffered.

Two Departures

1. Giraffes

The giraffes got away at dusk,
the pair of them headed for the zoo exit
along with the departing crowd—
two giants hardly seen against foliage in half-light
floating down the path among the trees,
their hooves frolicking out just as the gates were shut,

and the keepers chasing too late after into a deserted street
as the tall shapes faded in the dark air.

2. Giants

Out in the street the two giants
head home after work like everyone else
with rolled-up workclothes under their arms, holding
    lunchboxes,
and make their way to the train
that will take them to their nearby village:
It is Italy.

I was afraid, and ran ahead into a restaurant
and watched the approaching scene
from a table through the plate-glass window.
A gang of boys were following them down the street,
like they do in Italian towns,
attracted by the great misshapen bodies and knobby heads.
And as the giants turned off toward the railroad station,
no monsters but just workmen after all
living dull, hard-working, ordinary lives
(luckily there were two so they had each other),

the whole gang of boys streamed into the restaurant where I
was
and let them go on.

Four Poems Based on Eskimo Themes

1. A Fable of Disproportion

Once upon a time
a giant and a man were friends
and since wife-swapping was the custom then as now
they offered each other their wives for the night.

The man went to bed with the giant's wife
but he slipped and fell into her enormous cunt
where he dissolved, his bones
coming out in the flood when she pissed.

And when the giant screwed the man's wife
he split her in two and she lost her life.

2. The Great Farter

When the meat cache was frozen solid that winter
and we could not break it open,
we called on The Great Farter to help us.

We asked him to fart at the cache to loosen it.
I warn you, he said, if I fart on it
the meat will not be so tasty afterwards.

But what could we do? We had no other food,
so we kept on asking him and finally he did it,
he let off a tremendous fart at it,
and the blubber bags frozen into the ground,
which even hammering with stones had not budged,
burst wide open.

But the meat that was flung loose in every direction
now had such a smell we had to throw it away.

Not even the dogs would touch it,
it stank so from fart-smell.

3. Poontang

When I think of pussy
it makes me want to piss—
a push in the bush and it's
so warm and wet and squushy.

4. Beauty Cure

When I was just a girl
I once took a beauty treatment
recommended by our medicine man:
Grandma took me out
and found old dried-up dog turds for me.
I had to put each turd on my tongue
keeping it in my mouth until it was soft,
then rub myself with it
all over my breasts and stomach.
That is where I got my lovely figure and vitality from.
For as the medicine man said,
dogshit used in the right way
possesses magic powers
and is a kind of elixir of youth.
That is why I still look so young
in spite of my great age.
So for a beautiful complexion, ladies,
I do not hesitate to recommend dogshit lotion to you.
Try some today!

A Jew on Christmas

Hanukkah has its terrors as well as joys:
Not that we have to dread an annual slaughter anymore
with cossacks racing through Jewtown,
but now it is preparation for the period of sorrow that
    follows
when the Christians make a big fuss about Christmas
forcing us to admit that they enjoy themselves sometimes.
In other words it's not so bad to be a goy
and maybe it would even be fun to have a foreskin again,
risking infection, cheese, and the other well-known perils.

We usually keep our footing in the avalanche of Christmas
    cheer
but still Hanukkah gets buried
in spite of our renting Madison Square Garden and selling
    tickets.
Couldn't we circumcise Werner Von Braun on Christmas Day?

We try to take over with our genius for merchandising
but somehow living Jews are not as important as the dead
    one
and this is against our religion.
Say Kaddish for the dead, yes,
but to hold a wake with singing and drinking?
Drop dead, you Irishers.
Anyway it's a celebration for a Jew and that's what counts:
We've got all the goyim standing on their heads for one of
    ours.
(Come to think of it it's not a funeral, it's a birthday, so why
    does it feel like a funeral?)

Even Israel is sort of forgotten.
Now why are snow scenes supposed to be typical of
    Bethlehem?

Truly Christmas should feature Hebrew and palm trees,
with a rock from the Negev on every table
representing the barren and eternal
stone that rests in the soul of man.

When I walked down the streets of my hometown
and looked at the Christmas trees in the houses
(I liked the ones with all blue lights)
the ladies would sometimes call me in and give me candy
and tell me the story of virgin and child,
which I didn't doubt for surely my own mother had six.
Well, maybe the other five were fathered by that big schmuck
    named daddy
but I was the fruit of momma and God.
To tell the truth He is a worse father than daddy
because he scatters his children over the earth and lets
    them suffer
in the infinite ways of his mercy.

P.S. Now how did they dare call me dirty
when their own little bastard Jesus
was born in a stable reeking from animals
and to this day the whole story stinks of bullshit?

Jellyfish Invasion

each jellyfish being a colony
of cooperating organisms
it is amazing that one
is so much like another
like greek city states scattered
over the unruly land
some of the little creatures
like to play kidneys and others
are good for hearts
okay everybody join hands
and sing the national anthem

there must have been a time
when things were looser
a time between gas and solid
when things could shift about
imagine seeing through people
or whatever we were then
and hugging vapor to vapor
or jelly to jelly
that was an inventive time
this whole earth a big glob
and everyone shifting sex like mad
according to circumstance
and trying out different shapes like hats
lets get together and be dinosaurs gang
we do it now
but its like a tree trunk
trying to take a walk
better stay home
there are some things decided on

even the jellyfish is decided
each one has a constitution by plato

no poets wanted
this week a whole flock
sailed into reis park and the rockaways
like greeks in long ships
and won back the waters from the swimmers
troy fell and the trojans
fled screaming

Touriste de Banane by Georges Simenon

A boy, the unhappy kind Gerard Philippe played in the movies,
arrives at the tropical island from France—
Tahiti, unbelievably, is owned by France.

In a previous book this one is a sequel to
his family got involved in crimes of passion
and other front-page activities,
so the bourgeois structure of his life
was shattered by scandal and tragedy.

His plan now is to live in a deserted part of the island
(do unhappy boys always dream of this solution?),
but the Tahitian gendarmes are on the lookout
for people who saw Dorothy Lamour movies
and arrive to go native.
They are called banana tourists
because they think you can live off what grows wild,
but stagger back into town eventually
sick from malnutrition.

This boy manages to get away from town
and camps out efficiently in the wilderness, *très boyscout*,
where he makes the mistake of eating
an ordinary-looking but poisonous fish,
for in Tahiti as everywhere
nature lays traps for the innocent:
He nearly dies from it.

Worse, he broods about his life,
and recovering from the fish, he can't recover from his past.
(Of course I've been in analysis for fifteen years
and I'm still not over mine.)
Whatever happened in the previous book
must have been devastating

because even Tahiti, that garden of Eden, doesn't cure him.
Girls don't interest him much
and he doesn't seem to go for men:
He has evidently not been educated to pleasure.
There he sits in his jungle camp
with his mind on his miseries
as if he didn't have his whole life
to do with as he pleased.
Maybe he simply couldn't cope with all that freedom.
Him being French,
we can't be expected to understand his syndrome completely,
but we can try:

They grow up terribly polite, elegant and cold—all style,
shaking hands with each other like midgets
in short pants pulled up tight in the crotch.
Underneath they are desperate like we all are.
We Americans face our big crisis when we enter adolescence
but theirs occurs when they leave adolescence
with the idealism of the *lycée* guiding them
and they face the hard reality of what French life demands
    of an adult.
They are consoled perhaps by sex for losing love forever.
(But if you are not consoled
and commit a crime of passion, they understand
and you are not punished very hard, if at all.)

Our hero would never have been allowed
to follow his schoolboy fantasy to its tropic isle
had his family not all shot each other or something
and scandal wrecked his career.
To enter French life as an adult
you need the rigid definitions of your class to guide you
even as you fight them tooth and nail,
preferably on the Left Bank.

Without anything to rebel against,
allowed to live as French boys never are—as he wished—

he found growing up impossible
and knew he would never fit
into that elegant adult world of order and reason
he had been half-prepared for:
in a word, Paris.

And not being able to imagine any other thing worth doing
    with his life,
certainly not turning into a noble savage, even in Paradise,
he shot himself.

But I could have consoled you, Gerard,
why didn't you let me love you? Everyone thinks
as the lights go on and we get up and go out with the crowd.

But I could never have consoled you, we think twice on
    hitting the street,
having no room for such drama in my life,
and being no savior or prophet.
Each one teach one, UNESCO preaches,
and there is only strength for one
and that place in my heart is taken.
Besides, it is impossible to console a French boy in his
    metaphysical years.

And we head home to bed.

Graffiti

An Excerpt from *Sex Stories*

When the Men's Room was being demolished
to make way for a newer model, all steel and cement,
he broke in, holding his breath against the ancient stink,
and cut out an old wooden partition between the booths,
with its writings and pictures, and its glory holes,
some sealed repeatedly by the authorities
and others barely begun
where defects in the wood allowed pencil points to dig in
and one well-used one hacked out with knives and fingernails
with dried come encrusted on the rim
decorated with lips of mouth and cunt,
and around that, the cheeks of an ass;

and telephone numbers saying "call me"
and dates and times when free and where,
and descriptions of partners wanted
and acts or roles desired:
> *Sex slave, white, looking for black master*
> *Got a sister? Fix me up. Signed, Desperate*
> *Couple marié cherche troisième*
> *Have six hard inches meet me here tonight*
and true sex stories written out at length,
and instructive drawings of the sex organs in all positions
some half-washed out by the char, or painted over
but dug so deep or traced lovingly so often
they were still visible through the paint;
and still faintly seen but nearly overwhelmed at last,
the political slogans of past generations.

He took that whole wall, the size of a school blackboard,
figured over as it was like an oriental temple,
the work of a people, a folk artifact,

79

the record of lifetimes of secret desires,
the forbidden and real history of man,
and leaving it just as it was, hung it up in his house.

Respecting tradition
he charged everyone a nickel to see it.

Sharks

"In the forties the swan poem was obligatory, but in the sixties it is the shark poem."
—An overheard remark.

The shores are patrolled by sharks,
eastcoast and west alike.
Don't look, they're there all right,
and it's better not to see them
as you dunk yourself.

I'm so afraid of the sharky sea,
I know someday I'll wake up
and find myself floating in it
with bare toes.

How do the surfers dare
go so far out
with those toothy lurkers
in the waves?

Giant Pacific Octopus

I live with a giant pacific octopus:
He settles himself down beside me on the couch in the
 evening.
With two arms he holds a book
that he reads with his single eye:
He wears a pair of glasses over it for reading.

Two more arms go walking over to the sideboard across the
 room
where the crackers and cheese spread he loves are,
and they send back endless canapés, like a conveyor belt.

While his mouth is drooling and chomping,
another arm comes over and gropes me lightly:
It is like a breeze on my balls, that sweet tentacle.

Other arms start slipping around my body under my clothes,
they wiggle right in, one around my waist,
and all over, and down the crack of my ass.

I am drawn into his midst where his hot mouth waits for
 kisses
and I kiss him and make him into a boy
as all giant pacific octopuses are really
when you take them into your arms.

All their arms fluttering around you
become everywhere sensations of pleasure.
So, his sweet eye looks at me and his little mouth kisses me
and I swear he has the body of a greek god,
my giant pacific octopus boychik.

So this was what was in store
when I first saw him in the aquarium

huddled miserably on the rock
ignoring the feast of live crabs
they put in his windowed swimming pool.

You take home a creature like that, who needs love,
who is a mess when you meet
but who can open up like a flower with petal arms waving
    around—a beauty—
and it is a total pleasure to have him around,
even collapsible as he is like a big toy,
for as long as he will stay, one night or a lifetime,
for as long as god will let you have him.

Three Views of Eden:

1. The Expulsion

When last seen he was in a garden
frisking with the creatures and the plants.
He almost preferred the plants nowadays
with their stillness that never exhausted you
but somehow pumped you full of good air.

We drew a curtain of privacy over his life then
for even he has a right to a private life,
for a while anyway, although you know as well as I
that the world was going to call him again.
Some people are really public and he's one of them:

He'll have to come out of that garden he so loves
and step into the streets and join the throng
hurrying down to the central marketplace
where a throne and a gallows will be set up.
He'll be chosen, as his fate demands,
for one or the other, but never know which
until the trapdoor falls or the crown descends.

2. God Poem

Going out of my garden into the world of strangers
I don't ask for a great god's help,
I only ask a little one,
say the god of stones.

But invoking the small god
you risk intervention by a greater,
whether you want all that thunder and lightning or not.

84

Leave us in peace, great ones,
don't make us act out your cosmic dramas in our lives.

Why should we suffer that way
when all around us are the little gods, playful and ingenious,
a lot easier to live with than the roarers
who make us feel divine one minute
and rotten the whole rest of the year.

The trouble is that the shape of a small god
is a place a larger god can live in if he wants to.
But why should great Yahweh, bigshot,
crawl into my beloved god of stones
stretching his little face all awry
as he looms up into the heavens and darkens the sea
frightening some children playing on a lonely shore
who look up at his monster cloudshapes in the sky?

What choice have we got? None.
Life has put me out of my garden. I go.
Comfort me, stones.
Leaves like lips, speak to me.
Bug, let's race. You win darling.
Thank you little ones for the sweet moments.

Well, if great Yahweh descends
I have to don my hat and prayer shawl for him.

3. No To Eden

Eden was a garden all right
but none of my feelings had emerged yet
so it was like a book I was too young for.
There was no question of pleasure:
I even remember it as painful.

It was not the fruit of a tree that changed me then,
or rather it was all the fruits and flowers.
It was no snake alone,
but all the creatures were pointing in that direction:

I just never dreamed that it applied to me too.
But buds form and open in us like eyes
and suddenly different behavior is possible.
Why didn't that ever occur to me before, I thought,
and got up and walked away.

Everybody is like that, aren't they?
Even if we face failure and pain, we go;
we'd go in spite of everything.
The garden is stifling, that paradise,
and we go forth with vague heroic ideas
of fighting battles and winning the world.

We discover of course that we had it all wrong,
that life is very long as it races by,
that everything we vowed we'd never do, we do.
We have grown in the seven directions of the soul
and none of it is to be judged.

How simple life was before in the garden limits:
We sat in the sun and felt good,
it rained and we cried,
but we didn't have any choice in the matter.
Now we ache to see naked people,
on cold days sit in a hot bath for hours.
Can we raise the unlikely question,
Would I go back if I could?
Still I answer, No, to Eden.

Prognosis Negative

Waking up, and hoping as usual to feel good all over,
    this morning I have a sore neck;
    yesterday it was backache,
    sometimes half-voluptuous bowel problems,
or sex-wrecking disorders of the urinary tract:
    Everyday something.

To keep alive takes a larger army
    of servants and technicians every year,
until by the time you are ninety
    you are a miracle of science.
Your body like the headless man
    is connected to tubes at all the openings,
    purifying, feeding, keeping it all going
while a recorded voice repeats,
    "You are beautiful, you are adored."
Your environment becomes a machine
    regulating inflow, outflow, and overflow,
    with a head doctor running it all like an orchestra
        conductor.

Vitamins? They are understood, *ma chère,*
    like *service* in France is *compris*
    when a fat tip is still expected:
We get *en supplément* sheep embryo implants, mother's milk,
and, prescribed as necessary, monkey's balls.

There are fewer and fewer hours in the day
    one can afford to stay awake.
A young poet has come to sit at the master's feet.
The butler whispers,
    "He only receives from two to four now."
The bell rings:

You are injected with two hours of wakefulness,
    made up like Death in Venice
and wheeled out on a lounge into the salon.

The young poet sits as in a shrine.
    What you say will be admired, recorded and published.
What you think is:
    They are all handsome now, and so young (sigh), so
        young.
But only looking is allowed.
    You sip your one daiquiri as your eyes rove over him;
    mustn't waste a drop
for the total economy of the body is regulated
    and we're short of foreign exchange.

The alarm rings Time's Up, the specialists
    swarm out to make their various repairs,
and back you go
    into the half-sleep that keeps you alive.
"Work at forty
    so you won't be alone—and broke—at eighty."
Hopefully, we will be able to afford all that treatment.
    Don't count on Medicare, baby,
    which puts you in a ward on Welfare Island
    among the roaches and the poor
dragging your ass to the bathroom and eating the kind of
        chow
    guaranteed to kill off rather than prolong life
in the army of useless and unwanted
    put away there out of sight.

Already I have a general practitioner,
    a psychiatrist and a dentist
(not to speak of plain laborers all over the world
    raising my food, making my clothes,
    and chopping down whole forests for my paper alone).

As one by one my organs falter
    I will need a specialist in each
although now I'd like to be able to afford
        what seems the greatest luxury of all,
        a daily masseur. (And right this minute
couldn't I use someone with magic fingers
        on this sore neck and all the other places
        that need soothing and companionship.)

More and more I find myself susceptible to products
        that claim to give you zest and zoom,
        Z being the letter for life, even if kept in a zoo.
I want to follow zen diets, and believe in my heart
        that natural vitamins are superior to synthetic.
I am not prepared to get old, I say
        as I arrange my dwindling hairs over my forehead,
or any older even,
        although with the nations preferring war to peace
        and having those new blotto bombs,
the chances of a long life are slim for any of us.

There really is no preparing for the future
        (though don't knock money).
Still one must go on: Life is a struggle
        to get out of bed, a wise man said,
and it always seems to be morning again
        with no maid to bring me juice and coffee
and the daily masseur still
        a dream for the future.

The Tailspin

Going into a tailspin
in those days meant curtains.
No matter how hard you pulled back on the stick
the nose of the plane wouldn't come up.

Spinning round, headed for a target of earth,
the whine of death in the wing struts,
instinct made you try to pull out of it that way, by force,
and for years aviators spiraled down and crashed.

Who could have dreamed that the solution
to this dreaded aeronautical problem
was so simple?
Every student flier learns this nowadays:
You move the joystick in the direction of the spin
and like a miracle the plane stops turning
and you are in control again
to pull the nose up out of the dive.

In panic we want to push the stick away from the spin,
wrestle the plane out of it,
but the trick is, as in everything,
to go with the turning willingly,
rather than fight, give in, go with it,
and that way come out of your tailspin whole.